A KNIGHT WITH A BIG BLUE BALLOON

A KNIGHT WITH A BIG BLUE BALLOON

Ranjit Bolt

GIBSON SQUARE

This edition published for the first time by Gibson Square

UK   Tel: +44 (0)20 7096 1100
US   Tel: +1 646 216 9813

info@gibsonsquare.com
www.gibsonsquare.com

ISBN 9781783341382

Chapter titles are typeset in font Chocolate Covered Raindrops.

Papers used by Gibson Square are natural, recyclable products made from wood grown in sustainable forests; inks used are vegetable based. Manufacturing conforms to ISO 14001, and is accredited to FSC and PEFC chain of custody schemes. Colour-printing is through a certified CarbonNeutral® company that offsets its CO2 emissions.

Printed by CPI Group (UK) Ltd, Croydon CR0 4YY

Foreword

What should be the content of a limerick? This is a vexed question. It is certainly true that many people, if you say the word limerick, immediately think of something rude, or 'smutty', such as you might see scribbled on the wall in a public toilet. Bernard Shaw took the view that limericks simply had to be smutty, by definition. But Edward Lear, on the other hand, proved that this was not the case, producing many amusing examples.

Either way, how does a limerick work? How does it achieve its humorous effect. Apart from the comic sounds, I think a lot of the effect comes from the structure. A good limerick is structured rather like a joke. Generally speaking, the first two lines introduce the joke, and the third, fourth and fifth complete it. For example, take this classic one by Edward Lear:

> There was a young man from Nepal
> Who went to a fancy dress ball...

At this stage we are in suspense, waiting to see what absurd consequences will arise from this young man's decision to go to a fancy dress ball. Lines 3 – 5 answer the question, quite hilariously, as follows:

> He decided to risk it
> And went as a biscuit
> And a dog ate him up in the hall.

It is perhaps absurd effects like these – and the naturally comic sounds of English – that make the limerick a quintessentially British phenomenon.

My own love affair with the limerick began when I was a boy. I produced a few examples then, though I can't recall any of them. My interest was rekindled when, a while ago, I started writing them again and posting them on facebook to entertain friends. The response was very positive, with most of the limericks receiving a good smattering of 'likes'. The process proved therapeutic, and I believe it actually helped me to emerge from a bad period in my life.

Apart from the success of my limericks, I notice that a large national newspaper has a weekly limerick column. I am thrilled that the limerick itself at last seems to be enjoying a comeback in the twenty-first century!

sit vitiorum meorum evacuatio,
concupiscentiae et libidinis exterminatio,
caritatis et patientiae
humilitatis et obedientiae,
omniumque virtutum augmentatio.

Saint Thomas Aquinas

A knight with a big blue balloon

Blew it up like you blow a bassoon

And it swelled and it swelled

And he yelled and he yelled

As it carried him up to the moon.

A man in a restaurant in Sicily

Was eating his dinner quite prissily.

This behaviour was due

To the wild boar ragù

Which was horribly salty and gristly.

There was a young lady from Sharjah

Who mislaid her telephone charger

Which, I'll lay ten to one,

She would never have done

Had it been just a little bit larger.

There was a young lady named Hilton

Who was crazy for cheese and for Milton.

Drips of cheddar embossed

Her *Paradise Lost*

And her *Comus* was covered in stilton.

In her penthouse, a lady performer

Was rehearsing a number from 'Norma'

When she hit the top C

So indubitably

That it shattered the glass in the dormer.

A litotic fellow from Chile

Used terms that were terribly silly:

He called Hitler 'too bad',

King Lear 'frequently sad',

And the Andes 'in places quite hilly.'

There was a young man named Biddle

Who would miss when he went for a widdle

Every time he attempted

To get himself emptied

He left a great puddle of piddle.

The chief of the Wallakaleepee

Had become so incredibly sleepy

That the force of his snores

Almost shattered his jaws

And blew of the top of his teepee.

There once was a fellow named Cronin

Who would never, not ever, stop moanin'.

He'd have soon ceased to moan

If he'd only have known

That he simply had low serotonin.

There once was a woman named Whicker

Who had an affair with the vicar

Their liaison was short

Since the good father thought

It was sinful to kiss or to stroke her.

There was a young woman from Chinon

Whom the boys were incredibly keen on –

So pronounced were her charms

There were very few arms

That she hadn't at some point been seen on.

An unfortunate fellow from Salop

Dined at Scott's, where he ate a bad scallop,

And for days after that,

At the drop of a hat,

He'd be off to the loo at a gallop.

A top biological boffin

Retrieved a fresh corpse from its coffin

He brought it to life

And made it his wife

And now there's a kid in the offin'.

There was a young lady named Kirk

Whose special forte was to twerk.

Jaws would instantly drop,

Traffic come to a stop,

When she put her posterior to work.

A multigamous man from Saint Ives

Had a priceless collection of knives.

This was not meant for show

And, to prove it was so,

He had gutted all ten of his wives.

In a fresh electronic afflatus,

Every morning we post a new status,

And a harvest then comes

Of raised virtual thumbs

To assure us that people don't hate us.

A man I know called Keats

Is getting on my teats

On Facebook, the ponce,

Hasn't thumbed me up once

And he's retweeted none of my tweets.

If you're feeling the inverse of glee

That is cafard, or angst, or ennui

Try to think of a role

To rehearse in your soul

Of the people you're glad not to be.

There was a young lady from Sheen

Who kept brooding on what could have been,

But then, who does not?

It's everyone's lot,

Excepting perhaps for the queen.

There once was a drunkard from Hastings

Whose boozing earned constant lambastings,

Till, deterred by these drubs,

He avoided all pubs,

Though he totally caned it at tastings.

A chronic neurotic from Boulder

Felt Death's hand, day and night, on his shoulder.

'Soon I'll be on my way,'

He would constantly say,

As he kept getting older and older.

There was a young varmint called Nixon

Whom his schoolfellows kept playing tricks on

For the lad was, alas,

A right pain in the ass

And it's pains in the ass that one picks on.

A BBC bigshot called Chalmers

Made banal psychological dramas

Starring actors you've seen

Countless times on your screen

And with plots from the local embalmers.

There was a young man from Bulgaria

Whose behind just kept on getting hairier

Till a matted pelisse

Like a black weather's fleece

Covered all his posterior area.

There once was an MP called Menzies

Who must have been losing his senses

When he spent a whole week

With a tart on Mustique

Without putting it on his expenses.

Virgil, Dante and Milton made art

That I place in a class quite apart,

For they proved, for all time,

That the truly sublime

Can be reached by a boring old fart.

I've just finished a book by Flaubert

That's reduced me to virtual despair:

There's such bile in his quill

It has made me quite ill –

Pass the Rennies and give me some air!

Charles Baudelaire died of the clap

Van Gogh's madness was right off the map

Drink caused Thomas's death

Schubert ran out of breath

I'm so glad I'm an ordinary chap.

All of life is a matter of luck

And you don't get much bang for your buck:

You can wear overshoes,

Give up sat fats and booze –

And get squashed to a pulp by a truck.

The chef of an old king of Aragon

By his peers was considered a paragon,

Yet he died of remorse

For his béarnaise sauce

Always had just a tad too much tarragon.

An old Frankish princess named Bertha

Had so massive and monstrous a girth, a

Team of twenty-two big

Strong young men on a dig

Took a week and a half to unearth her.

When I feel like John Clare in 'I Am'

I just reach for the diazepam

And in less than two ticks

It'll totally fix

My desire to jump into the Cam.

The past doesn't need to be good,

Though it might be quite nice if it could.

All it needs is to go

And it's bathed in a glow

Like the sunlight you get in a wood.

There was a young fellow from Hayes

Who suffered from constant malaise.

Asked the cause of his woes

He replied: 'I suppose

It's this endless succession of days.'

Epicurus said, 'If you aspire

To be happy, then limit desire.'

So I've given up flakes,

Drinking, women, and steaks,

And my life's become utterly dire.

There once was an art nut named Bodden

Who would weep when he looked at a modern.

Seeing Rothkos, or Pollocks,

Although they were bollocks,

His hanky was sure to be sodden.

There was a sad fellow from Spain

Who, like cotton, would shrink in the rain

Which was probably why

He came home one foot high

After taking a stroll on the plain.

A very old man from Iraq

Was one hundred per cent in the dark

As to why his home town

Got completely knocked down

By a plane that could not miss its mark.

There was once a contrarian cat

Who sat anywhere else but the mat

They said: 'That's not condign

Don't you know the old line?'

And the cat answered: 'Yaboo to that!'

There was a poor fellow from Tulsa

Who had picked up a permanent ulcer

Having borne, all his life,

The assaults of his wife

While lacking the strength to repulse her.

A colonel who fought hard in Crimea

Got a dreadful attack of diarrhoea

When, with speed and precision,

A Russian division

Attacked his brigade in Fodosiya.

There once was a stripper from Strood

Whose act was disgracefully rude

For she liked to unloose

A great tide of abuse

On the tossers by whom she was viewed.

There once were some Carmelite nuns

Who were famed for their firm curvy buns.

You will ask, how did they bake them

Or wiggle and shake them?

But I never unravel my puns.

There was once a large lady from Mull

Who was built like a galleon's hull

She expired prematurely

When (tragically, surely)

They had an obesity cull.

There once was a poet named Bevan

Whose prosody stank to high Heaven.

I might cite his heptameters

Which so leapt their parameters

Some had ten feet, some even eleven.

There once was a young man called Jude

Who was quite the definitive pseud:

Not one play had he seen

Save to say that he'd been

And he went to a view to be viewed.

An ascetic, now centuries dead,

Dined on nothing but water and bread

Though I'm told that he would,

If he'd been really good,

Swap his nails for an ordinary bed.

Geoffrey Chaucer'd completed a poem

For the king, that he wanted to show 'im.

At the end he cried: 'Fuck!

Yet again I get stuck

On the envoi! I murdered the proem!'

There was once a wise man from Cadiz

Who concluded that life is a swiz:

Day succeeds dreary day

But you still want to stay

As it seems to be all that there is.

If you're gloomy, and life isn't funny,

First, suspect that you've mislaid some money,

Then recall where it went,

And on what it was spent,

And you'll be a much happier bunny.

English literature always drew torrents

Of abuse from my old auntie Florence:

She'd a loathing of Shaw,

An aversion to Waugh

And an utter abhorrence for Lawrence.

There was once a collector called Hubbard

And you should have just heard how he blubbered

On discovering a crack

Going right down the back

Of a hundred grand Louis Quinze cupboard.

An old troubadour from Seville

As a poet did not fit the bill

His ballads all stank

His sonnets were rank

And his villanelles made people ill.

The past has gone, vanished, vamoosed,

In no way can it be reproduced.

If you find this unfair,

And you've ten years to spare,

Then you might want to try reading Proust.

When they noticed Pope Leo's strange squirms

And enquired, in quite tentative terms,

Why he wriggled all day

'Wouldn't you?' he would say

'If you'd started a Diet of Worms?'

A certain young lady from Malta

Was so gorgeous you just couldn't fault her

Half the guys in Valetta

Their own arms would fetter

In case they should try to assault her.

Venice; poker; old friends; scrambled eggs;

A woman with wonderful legs;

Shakespeare's plays; Handel's airs;

Anything of Baudelaire's

And a Château Margaux (minus dregs).

There was one final fellow named Cass

Who was truly a pain in the ass

I would try to make clear

His annoyingness here

But there aren't enough swear words, alas.

A Parisian banker named Reine

Went too long of the dollar and yen

And it has to be said

There weren't many tears shed

When he threw himself into the Seine.

A wealthy investor from Fife,

When sent a prospectus for Life

Plc, said: 'No way!

This is not going to pay –

The main products are Trouble and Strife.'

There was a young man from Mauritius

Who was captious, uncouth, and officious.

This was somewhat allayed

By a lamb stew he made

Which was utterly fucking delicious.

In my youth, on a permanent roller,

Still I didn't know crap from Shinola.

Now I'm old, grey, and wise,

Life has opened my eyes,

But I'm weary, and broke, and bipolar.

An old fromager of Coutances

Was a pain in the ass and a ponce,

But to pick up the smell

Of his best Neufchâtel

Was to pardon his failings at once.

Tracey looked in the mirror, and said:

'No sane bloke's gonna go near my bed –

Not with that kinda face –

It's just taking up space –

It can go to Tate Modern instead.'

A canny wee lass from Culodden

Took a dog do in which she had trodden;

Used a chisel to mould it

And eventually sold it

For twelve million quid to Tate Modern.

Virgil, Wordsworth – longueurs by the score,

Proust and Tolstoy – so often a bore,

Milton, pompous as fuck,

Dante – Canto I – stuck –

What the hell is great literature for?

If you languish in Saturn's dark power

And your gloom's getting worse by the hour

There's a time-honoured cure

That's as swift as it's sure:

Take a ten-minute freezing cold shower.

Once I went to a sadhu named Seth

Who'd discovered the answer to death:

'The solution,' he said,

Sagely nodding his head,

'Is never to breathe your last breath.'

Having boarded the bus of despair

And handed the driver my fare,

I said: 'Take me to Hell –

If I don't ring the bell

Could you give me a shout when we're there?'

There was once a logician named Ruth

Who was vexed by the nature of Truth

But she certainly knew

That her suffering was true

When she got a huge hole in her tooth.

A Samian soldier's got my shield –

I dropped it when I quit the field.

Why should I worry?

Shields are rife,

Whereas I've only got one life.

I woke up just now and thought: 'Golly!

It's Christmas – I've GOT to be jolly,'

But I've sat on my knackers,

Mislaid all the crackers

And just pricked my thumb on sodding holly!

To the neutral, the straight, and the queer,

Those I don't know, and those I hold dear,

To the short and the tall,

To the big and the small,

May I wish an amazing New Year.

There once was a painter called Durer

Whose genius could not have been purer

And the fact that he's great

Can be seen from the rate

His collectors must pay the insurer.

Two old Scotsmen from round John O'Groats

Said, while nervously casting their votes:

'They've got Churchill, the Bard,

Newton, stars by the yard,

We've got Hume, haggis, oil, and boiled oats!'

There was a young lady from Brussels

Who possessed the most marvellous muscles

But I'm sorry to say

There was rank disarray

'mid her neurons and glands and corpuscles.

There was once a cantankerous bug

Who, as bugs go, was rather a thug:

If another bug riled it,

Or mocked, or reviled it,

He'd give it a punch in the mug.

In England, befriending one's neighbours

Is like one of Hercules' labours –

Just to say 'How d'ye do.'

Or to borrow a screw

Is like lifting eleven huge cabers.

There was a young lady from Oakham

Who would go up to people and poke 'em.

If they were awake

They would cry: 'For Pete's sake!'

And if they were sleeping it woke 'em.

There was a young man from Sardinia

Who got skinnier and skinnier and skinnier.

This depleted his strength

And it meant that at length

He resembled the stalk of a zinnia.

There once was a fellow named Hoople

Who to bib and to booze didn't scruple

And where we might have trouble

Merely ordering a double

He would happily have a quadruple.

Our wealth distribution is feudal,

We're reviled as America's poodle,

Our climate is rain,

More rain, rain yet again,

And we were run by a public school noodle

Sometimes life leaves me right in the dark –

Take the loss of the great Warren Clarke,

Who, as cool as you please,

And with consummate ease,

Kicked the bulk of his peers round the park.

I was always a sceptical sod

To whom faiths of all kinds seemed quite odd,

But when Clarkson was sacked

I did know, for a fact,

That there is a benevolent God.

When Ed learned, with the polling complete,

That Labour'd been left with one seat

In a Tory landslide

'Bloody Nora!' he cried

'That's the last bacon butty I'll eat.'

When Farage was informed that some frogs

Had been shot by a couple of wogs

So infarcted was he

Both with fury and glee

That he finished up popping his clogs.

There once was a young man from Wapping

Who went on for three hours without stopping.

Now you think I'm being rude

But you've quite misconstrued –

It was only some wood he was chopping.

A curious fellow named Bate

Would constantly cachinnate.

When his wife kicked the bucket

He cried: 'Yaboo suck it!'

And he hasn't stopped laughing to date.

There once was a fellow called Young

Who would never stop brushing his tongue.

He went time after time

At the gunk and the slime

But still they persistently clung.

I once saw a shrink named Goswami,

Having gone almost totally barmy.

'I can cure you,' he said,

As I kicked in his head.

'Yeah, right,' I said, 'you and whose army?'

A gloomy old chap from the Ruhr

Once went to a shrink for a cure,

But the shrink simply said:

'Are you clean off your head?

There is only one cure – to endure.'

A miserable bugger called Fink

Decided to go to a shrink.

But the shrink simply said:

'From your birth till you're dead

Life is horrible – what did you think?'

A poorly depressive from Lyme

Learned from doctors he hadn't much time.

'It's malignant,' they said,

'In three months you'll be dead.'

'Then, in my book,' he said, 'it's benign.'

One recalls through a soft-focus haze

One's old university days

Having neatly expunged

All the times one was plunged

In a mire of appalling malaise.

It is only this minute that counts

And the rest don't matter an ounce –

If a beast lies in wait

In the guise of our fate

Let it pick its own moment to pounce.

I use a trebuchet

To smash my cares away

Its power's immense

It's common sense

And it triumphs pretty much every day.

Life is nasty and brutish and short,

Or that is what Thomas Hobbes thought.

Nasty? Wouldn't demur –

Brutish? Wholly concur –

But the short bit I never quite bought.

For Churchill it came as a dog,

For John Bunyan a slough (or a bog),

Samuel Johnson knew best,

Who, when HE got depressed,

Simply downed a few bottles of grog.

When your worries are starting to win

You must not take their crap on the chin –

Just try rolling them all

Into one single ball

And then bunging the ball in the bin.

A manic depressive called Leigh

Was prescribed some CBT.

So he looked at his life,

Just saw sorrow and strife,

And threw himself into the sea.

To conk out in the early AM,

And not have to wake up again,

Is the best gift the gods

(Those vindictive sods)

Will ever bestow upon men.

Sorrow's partly its own self-begetter –

Roughly 50 per cent of it's 'meta':

Try to be less aware

That you're in such despair

And you're likely to feel a bit better.

You're a fusser, a fretter, a minder

To whom life could have been a lot kinder?

Try to see it this way:

If you got through the day

Then you just played an absolute blinder.

You can search like there's no tomorrow,

You can beg, or steal, or borrow,

And find nothing as fair –

No, no beauty so rare

As that of a face bathed in sorrow.

When one's feeling all flummoxed and flustered

And one's life isn't cutting the mustard

One just opens one's wings

And hopefully sings,

Like a tit, or a tern, or a bustard.

Among my most paramount aims,

Before I'm consigned to the flames,

Is to quite comprehend,

From beginning to end,

Just one sentence of late Henry James.

Kiss goodbye to my greed and my lust,

You will not see my failings for dust,

I'll be kind, never grumble,

None so pliant or humble,

From hereon on it's heaven, or bust!

A depressive from Danzig called Gödel

Found the whole of existence a hurdle.

He would look at the day

Breaking over the bay

And his blood would immediately curdle.

A very vain tenor called Carter

To his bowels was an absolute martyr

And it tore him apart

When he did a loud fart

At the start of the Coffee Cantata.

There once was a fellow called Vasey

Who was mad about chicken jalfrezi

If you went to the loo

And he'd been before you

The aroma could drive you half crazy.

There once was a bishop of Nantes

Who went for a wee in the font –

He was deeply contrite

But God said, 'It's all right

You can dump in it too if you want.'

There was young fellow from Deal

Who had buttocks as rigid as steel

And wherever he went

The fair ladies of Kent

Would accost him and give them a feel.

I once met a couple called Pooter

Who were neither male, female, nor neuter.

I'm not sure what they were

But can safely aver

That few bottoms I've seen have been cuter.

Irreverent

A Merseyside lass named Corinna

Pulled a bloke from Belgrade at a dinner

And it thus could be said

That, though from Birkenhead,

She'd a great deal of Serbian in her.

A lady on board the Titanic

Saw it sinking and swiftly grew manic

First she prayed to the Lord

Then of men still aboard

Bedded a hundred and three in her panic.

When a hideous fellow from Conques

Asked a girl he'd just met for a bonk

Her rejoinder was this:

'Please don't take it amiss

But I'd sooner be thrown off Mont Blanc.'

A lady who lived in Twin Cities

Was incredibly proud of her titties

Every day when she woke

She would give them a poke

And say: 'How are you doing, my pretties?'

A lovely young lady named Cunningham

Could go nowhere near guys without stunning 'em.

They would line up ten deep

On the beach, for a peep

At her naughty bits while she was sunning 'em.

There once was a lady called Toya

Who could not have been primmer or coyer

If you asked her her name

She'd turn crimson with shame

While a hand on her knee would destroy her.

An escort who worked out of Nottingham

Gave her johns extra kicks by garrotting 'em;

Since they left with their faces

Still purple in places

The vice squad had no trouble spotting 'em.

There was a young girl from Des Moines

Who dressed in a skirt made of coins

Till a moment of lust

When she rolled in the dust

And they rattled away from her loins.

There was a young man from Arbroath

Who attempted to sleep with a sloth.

They were into foreplay

When the branch came away

With disastrous results for them both.

The chef of a hotel in Thame,

While chopping shallots, missed his aim;

Though the guests still got fed

His performance in bed

From that moment was never the same.

An Edwardian woman from Dorset

Could never quite fasten her corset

If her husband should try

She would stop him and cry:

'Ye will burst me balloons if ye force it!'

An old Goth kept his whole nation busy –

They would ask one another: 'Who is he?

He helped to sack Rome,

But Ravenna's his home –

Is the old bugger Ostro or Visi?'

There was a young lady called Meg

Whose life was a real curate's egg –

She had millions in trust,

A fantabulous bust,

But only one arm and one leg.

There once was a tart from Smyrna

Whose behind was the kind of head-turner

That Rodin or Canova

Would have fairly drooled over,

Besides being a nice little earner.

A man from Martinique

Had lost one buttock cheek

For a buzzard had swooped

From the sky while he pooped

And had carried it off in its beak.

For a cute Russian actress called Litov

With directors it never would hit off.

For as hard as they pleaded

That nude scenes were needed

No way was she taking her kit off.

A girl from East Langdon near Dover

Had a shag in a field full of clover

The sex was first rate

Unbelievably great

But she came away purple all over.

A fellow from Bagnor near Newbury

Got a big purple lump on his do-berry;

When he first saw it there

He cried: 'Well, I declare!

Is that herpes, or merely a blueberry?'

There was a young lady from Venice

Who was good at two things: sex and tennis

And, as one would have thought,

When she got on the court

She was really a bit of a menace.

There was a young lady called Futter

Who was really a bit of a nutter.

She could only enjoy

Making love to a boy

If he'd swathed her in oodles of butter.

A fickle old sculptor called Weaver

Was obsessed with his young lover's beaver.

He so craved it, that once

He had cast it in bronze

So he'd still have it there, should he leave her.

A girl violinist from Rio

Played with two randy guys in a trio

If things started to slump

She would just bear her rump

And they'd both begin playing con brio.

There once was a girl from Saint Kitts

Who had the most fabulous tits

Merely glimpsed from afar

If not wearing her bra

She could drive a guy out of his wits.

There was a young lady from Dallas

Who was quite psychopathically callous –

If she went off a guy

'stead of saying goodbye

She would bite off the poor blighter's phallus.

There was a young fellow from Brighton

Who was terribly easy to frighten –

Cock a snook, or say 'Boo!'

That was all you need do

For his scrotum to instantly tighten.

There was a young man from South Tees

Whose cute bottom drove girls off their trees

But its merits were marred

By its being so hard

It was actually painful to squeeze.

A lady from Abergavenny,

For some reason, was not getting any,

So she moved to Porthcawl

And erected a stall

Where she touted herself for a penny.

There was a young Scotsman named Jock

Who was having a swim in a loch

When he raised a great shout

And came scurrying out

With a crayfish attached to his cock.

A willy upbraided its owner

For being so much of a loner:

'It's rather a bore

And it's making me sore

There's a tart round the corner, please phone her.'

There was a young girl from Stranraer

Whose boobs were too big for her bra.

I would finish this, but

I've regaled you with smut

And I don't want to push it too far.

60

There was a young man from Lake Placid

Whose thing was a foot long when flaccid,

If you'd seen it erect

You'd have first double checked

And then thought you were tripping on acid.

A lady from Poland called Lottie

Drove all the Cracovians potty

Because a) she'd a bod

That was given by God

And b) she would shag for a zloty.

There was a young man from Provence

Who was mad about Anatole France

And if someone appeared

With a long pointy beard

He would adjust his trousers at once.

There was a young lady from Lydd

Who was good at whatever she did

If she did the whole lot

She was so incredibly hot

It'd set you back five hundred quid.

A randy young lady from Kent

Wanted bedding wherever she went

And she even had got

A tattoo on her ****

Saying: 'Fanny, for sale or to rent.'

There was a young man from Milwaukee

Who was quite understandably cocky

Being blessed with a dong

So thick, rigid and long

That it could have been used to play hockey.

There was a young girl from of Rangoon

Whose bod would make any guy swoon

It is making me come

Just to *think* of her bum

And her boobs could be seen from the moon.

There was an old woman from Glamis

Who had surgically salvaged her charms

And at seventy-four

There were guys by the score

Who would bed her without any qualms.

There once was a Lancashire lass

Who would have you whatever your class.

Baron, banker or trucker

Was welcome to bed her

As long as he had a nice ass.

A modest Scots lassie named Hannah

Only coupled in the missionary manner.

If you ever suggested

Some new way be tested

Her answer was: 'Och, no! I canna!'

A lady from Leamington Spa

On first dates never went very far

You could addle your wits

Trying to fondle her tits

For a schtup you could wish on a star.

A frustrated young man from Torquay

Once tried shagging a hole in a tree

But by awfully bad luck

First his willy got stuck

Then it was had by a squirrel for tea.

There was a young lady from Goa

Who let nobody biblically know her

So when horniness struck

In the place of a ****

She would tickle her cat with a boa.

There was a young man from Hong Kong

Who insisted on wearing a thong

Though the way it would pass

Up the crack of his ass

Made him wriggle and squirm all day long.

There was a young lady named Greta

Who would charge to let anyone pet her

You could have a good feel

For the price of a meal

And for two you could thoroughly vet her.

As the blood was beginning to trickle

From the crotch of my gardener, Pickle,

I promptly drew near

Whereupon it was clear

That he'd cut off his knob with his sickle.

There once was a fellow called Fitches

Whose knob was too big for his breeches

If a woman went by

And she gave him he eye

He would finish up bursting the stitches.

A shy girl from Cas Troggi

Would only shag when the weather was foggy

And when it was clear

She would proffer her rear

And insist upon doing it doggy.

When she got the itch, Lady Godiva

Paid a serf or a servant to swive her

And their usual quote

Was no more than a groat

(Which in modern-day money's a fiver).

A certain young gay man from Tring

Who kept putting rings in his thing

Had so many at last

That when at half-mast

It looked less like a cock than a spring.

There was a young man called McNutty

Who covered his thing in putty,

But, for better or worse,

I can't finish this verse

As the end is appallingly smutty.

There was a young fellow from Dallas

Who could not keep his hands off his phallus:

Where his right hand had been

There was now to be seen

Just a huge, irremovable callus.

An old man from Soucy-En-Brie

Was as stoic as stoic can be:

You could rip out his guts,

Slap his wife, squash his nuts,

And all he would say was: 'Tant pis.'

There was a young lady from Tring

Who bedizened her belly with bling.

At the height of her joys

People thought that the noise

Was the telephone starting to ring.

An Irish ex-con named O'Rorke

Had a rather peculiar walk;

When they asked him 'How come?'

He said: 'I blames me bum

And a long stretch in prison in Cork.'

There was a young man named MacDowell

Who slept several times with an owl.

This may not be believed

But the owl, it conceived –

The result was a curious fowl.

There was a young lady named Neam

Who slept with a goat in a dream

But on waking she found

The same goat still around –

Now she's got seven kids and free cream.

There was a young lady from Floors

Who kept dislocating her jaws;

When the dentist enquired

Whence the damage transpired

'Is he...?' 'Yes,' she replied, 'like a horse!'

There was an old man from Strathclyde

Who purchased a Latvian bride

Being willing and eager

Like some girls from Riga

She shagged him all night and he died.

There was an old lecher from Leicester

Who met a cute lass and possessed her

He was proud as a lord

To have bagged such a broad

Till his genitals started to fester.

A sick lady arch-deacon called Proctor

Had a steamy affair with her doctor.

It was great, out of sight,

They made love day and night,

Till the bishop found out and defrocked her.

There was an old man from Dumfries

Who was fond, not of goose, but of geese –

Every day during autumn

He'd woo 'em and court 'em

Till someone informed the police.

There was a young lady from Ghent

Who would only be bedded for Lent –

She'd be fondling away

Pretty much night and day

While the rest of us tried to repent.

There was a young housewife from Frome

Who would bring herself off with a broom

And no woman alive

Had been known to derive

So much pleasure from sweeping a room.

There was a young man from Brize Norton

Who would have his wife with the sport on

As he rogered her whole,

If his team scored a goal,

His reaction was not to be thought on.

A penurious scholar named Barrett

Kept a rabbit upstairs in his garret

This went horribly wrong

When it mistook his dong

For some curious species of carrot.

'All sex is a sin' was the credo

Of a lady who lived in Toledo

And to make it secure

And keep herself pure

She stuffed her *chumino* with playdough.

There was a young man from La Plata

Who insisted that size didn't matter

But in secret each day

He would kneel down and pray

For his *chota* to be longer and fatter.

A man from the mountains called Andy

Was so inconceivably randy

He would willingly sleep

With a goat or a sheep

If a chap or a lass wasn't handy.

A bashful young lady from Reach

Had been sunning herself on the beach

She was brown as a nut

Save her boobs and her butt

Which still looked like she'd soaked them in bleach.

Every day, as the sun 'gan to wester,

A Medieval lady from Leicester

Would retire for the night

And be bedded out of sight

By her sumpter, her reeve and her jester

There was a young lady from Warwick

Whom the orders could make quite euphoric:

Of Corinthian she crooned,

For Ionic she swooned,

And she came like a train over Doric.

There was a young man from the Bronx

Who hadn't been seen to in yonks

Till at length the poor fellow

Sought out a bordello

And had seven consecutive bonks.

There once was a man named McWatters

Who was mad about beavers and otters

But this penchant of his

Got the law in a tiz

And they put him in prison, the rotters.

A young married man from Fife

Would consistently bugger his wife.

When he asked her one day:

'Shall we try t'other way?'

She said: 'Sodomy? Not on your life!'

There was a young banker from Luton

Who could only have sex with his suit on;

He would undo his flies

And part his wife's thighs

And they'd bonk till they'd broken the futon.

A lady who lived in Grenoble

Gave up sex but would sometimes wobble.

She'd go out in the street

And the first man she'd meet

She'd unzip and go down on and gobble.

There was a young lady called Cora

Who made all her girlfriends adore her.

I'd best not say how,

Or leastways not now,

(It required a courgette and some Flora).

To a Scotsman I once knew named Warren

The whole notion of undies was foreign –

This he tended to find

Quite a bit of a bind

As his balls were too big for his sporran.

There was a young lady from Stoke

Who was not very nice to her bloke.

Just one Friday in two

She'd allow him a screw

Even that was a cursory poke.

There was a young lady from Burma –

Total knock-out is how I should term her:

Her behind was as round

As a new-minted pound

And her breasts were like melons, but firmer.

There was an old flasher called Burke

Who would go to the forest and lurk.

There, as dusk would descend,

You might glimpse his rear end,

Like a miniature moon in the murk.

There once was a man from the Bronx

Who possessed the most vocal of conks

During sex it was worst

For then from it would burst

A whole gamut of bellows and honks.

There was a young girl from King's Lynn

Whose titties were made out of tin

And whenever she ran

Or was touched by a man

They emitted one Hell of a din.

There once was a young lady actor

Who'd contrived to stay *virgo intacta*

Though she'd got several parts

Shared a flat with two tarts

And had three rich old codgers who backed her.

A passionate lady called Mame

Once hollered so loud when she came

That the windows all broke

Which delighted her bloke

Though his hearing was never the same.

There was a young lady named Bisset

Whose passes were strictly implicit:

She would give you some cue

That she wanted a screw

But you just had to blink and you'd miss it.

One fine evening a lady from Norway

Told her other half, 'Let's do it your way.'

'Are the fetters too tight?'

He enquired with delight

As she hung there stretched out in the doorway.

There was a young man from Uganda

Whose thing was a massive four-hander

But this badly backfired

When a servant expired

As he bedded her on the veranda.

There was also a man from West Sheen

Whose balls were the size of a bean

And whenever he came

It was always the same:

There was barely semen to be seen.

There was a young housewife from Schilda

Who jumped into bed with her builder

And so long and so thick

Was this gentleman's prick

That their intercourse damned nearly killed her.

There was a young lady from Louth

Whose tongue, as it headed due south,

Would so skillfully lick

She could swallow your prick

While you weren't quite yet in her mouth.

A Hispanic escort from Topeka

Got to Congress, the clever young *chica*,

But in less than a day

They had turned her away

For performing an act on the Speaker.

A randy young lady named Laing

Stopped at nothing in quest of a bang

She once took two men

To the top of Big Ben

Where she came with a boom and a clang.

A fastidious man named Killkuddy

Rather fancied the bird of his buddy

One fine day in a field

She was ready to yield

But he hated to get his clothes muddy.

There once was a woman named Mabel

Who was madly in love with Clark Gable

Till he gave her a rash

At a Hollywood bash

When they shagged on the billiard table.

The second Marchese di Dondola

Once tried to have sex in a gondola

But the serf he had chosen

Was distant and frozen

And barely allowed him to fondle her.

There was a young man from Dunblane

Who could only get pleasure from pain

The most tender caress

Turned him on ten times less

Than a welt from a whip or a cane.

There was a young lady from Hyde

Who, of all the positions she'd tried,

Liked her partner below her

And, being a goer,

A girlfriend along for the ride.

There was a young pervert named Fred

Who liked to be tied to the bed

With a clamp round his knob

And a gag in his gob

And a shopping bag over his head.

There was a young lady from Kettering

Whose sexual techniques took some bettering

She was so terribly hot

That tattooed on her ****

She had 'SHAG ME AND DIE' in red lettering.

An adventurous pervert named Rix

Stinted not in pursuit of his kicks

He'd had goats, sheep, an elk,

An extremely large welk

And not one armadillo but six.

A Germanist prof named Roberta

Would inveigle her students to hurt her.

She could once hardly walk

After giving a talk

On the links between Byron and Goethe.

There was a young fellow named Lambton

Who used to play prop for Northampton

But he couldn't quite stick it

And moved on to cricket

Where willies get hit, but not stamped on.

An Istanbul tart named Samira

Would have you for one Turkish lira

And what she would do

If you went up to two

Isn't fit for the filthiest hearer.

I once paid a call on a whore

Who had 'Strict Mistress' pinned to her door

By the time we were done

I'd had oodles of fun

But cor blimey my bottom was sore.

There was a young fellow named Sykes

Who had curious sexual likes

Just a glimpse of a chain

Would drive him insane

To say nothing of collars and spikes.

There was a young fellow from March

Whose pyjamas were stiffer than starch.

Asked to comment, he said:

'If I'd only got wed

They'd be pliant and sprung as a larch.'

While at Balliol, Lady Godiva,

Though she'd been an inveterate skiver,

Still so tickled the fools

Of the monks at the Schools

That she easily sailed through her *viva*.

A musical lady named Shoonah

Had a fling with her harpsichord tuner

His erotic technique

Knocked her into next week

And she came like a train, only sooner.

There was a young woman from Ayr

Who had acres of thick pubic hair

So that finding her ****

Was a bit of a hunt

Though one had to assume it was there.

There once was a girl from Mauritius

Whose morals were sordid and vicious.

Female critics weren't kind

But the men didn't mind

Since her figure was simply delicious

A young music-lover named Dom

Picked up his new bird at a Prom.

This she'll never regret

Or she hasn't done yet

For his plonker is plied with aplomb.

There was once a young fellow from Riga

Who was ready and willing and eager

But, I'm sad to relate,

His desire was as great

As his willy was floppy and meager.

A young lady's behaviour got risky

After one fairly sizeable whisky

After one or two more

It got worse; after four

There was no girl in England as frisky.

There was once a young fellow from Ongar

Who was built just like Ajax, but stronger

He'd lift twice his own weight

And I scarcely need state

That no lover could keep it up longer.

A lady from Falmouth called Sookie

Had a sexual aplomb that was spooky

What she did for a joke

To one innocent bloke

Led to people being spattered in Newquay.

There was a young lady named Gerda

For whom nooky was absolute murder

You may find this absurd

And not credit my word

But you would if you'd been there and heard her.

A horny young couple named Baines

Were mad about shagging in trains

Once, they got on at Crewe

And were still in the loo

When they stopped two hours later at Staines.

There was a young girl from Malpensa

Who had boobs like balloons, but immenser –

So far out did they jut

In a dress of low cut

She provided a case for the censor.

An inveterate lecher from Bicester

Was insanely in love with his sister.

This compounded his sins

And played Hell with his shins

As she kicked him whenever he kissed her.

A randy young devil named Doug

Was bedding his girl on the rug

When her dog butted in

And began bonking him

Thank the Lord it was only a pug.

There was a young Scotsman named Hannah

Who sat by mistake on a spanner

As he hollered 'Hoots mon!'

Both his nuts were undone

Now he wants to have kids but he canna.

An unfortunate fellow named Gore

Fell insanely in love with a whore,

And much good it did –

She charged two hundred quid

And he finished up paying her four.

There was also a lady called Lana

Who had found a new path to Nirvana.

I would like to say what

But perhaps I'd best not

(Just think sizeable unripe banana).

A lady from Leamington Spa

Had the biggest known bosoms by far

They were so massive that

Two grown men and a cat

Could have sailed round the world in her bra.

There was a young girl from Manhattan

Who made love on a mattress of rattan

With such force did she come

It imprinted her bum

With a permanent latticework pattern.

There was one final fellow from Crewe

Who spent most of his life on the loo

He would push, he would shove

Pray to Heaven above

But mere pebbles at best would ensue.

There was a young lady called Zimmer

Whose libido was barely a glimmer

But I happen to know

This would not have been so

Had her husband been just a tad slimmer.

There was a young fellow named Eddie

Whose behaviour was somewhat unsteady

He would prance round the town

With his pants hanging down

And his thirteen-inch thing at the ready.

A lovely young typist from Shotham

Had a quite unbelievable bottom.

On a full morning train

(Which it was, in the main)

Blokes would frequently pinch it, God rot 'em!

An amazing young hottie named Meryl

Had six piercings downstairs made of beryl

And though fellas would queue

For the chance of a screw

They accomplished that aim at their peril.

An unfortunate lass from Atlantis

Had a brush with a small praying mantis

Of a quite vicious kind

Which nipped her behind

As she put on her mythical panties.

There was a young man from Manila

Who was hung like a second Godzilla.

So immense was his bone

That the men who built Rome

Could have used it instead of a pillar.

There was once a young woman from Burma

Super-sexy is how I should term her

When she walked through Rangoon

All the fellas would swoon

As their willies grew firmer and firmer.

There was a young lady called Tina

Whose fanny could not have been cleaner

Till, by fearful mishap,

She bedded a chap

With ketchup on the end of his wiener

I've discovered a note by Leigh Hunt

As authoritative as it's blunt:

They'd drug Dorothy's beer,

Coleridge came from the rear,

While Wordsworth went in at the front.